To

....

From

....

My prayer for you . . .

....

The Lord listens when I pray to him.

—Psalm 4:3

Dedicated to the prayer warriors of
Rapha God Ministries.
May God hear every word you say to Him.
And may you hear every word He says to you.

—Max & Denalyn Lucado

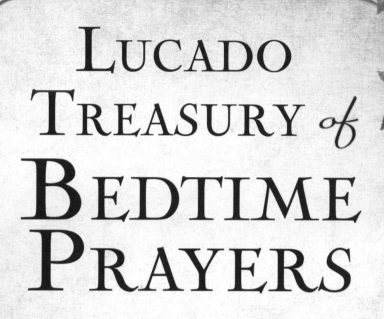

Lucado Treasury of Bedtime Prayers

*Prayers for bedtime
and every time of day!*

with original prayers

BY MAX & DENALYN LUCADO

ILLUSTRATED BY LISA ALDERSON

A Division of Thomas Nelson Publishers

NASHVILLE   MEXICO CITY   RIO DE JANEIRO

© 2015 by Max & Denalyn Lucado

Karen Hill, Executive Editor for Max Lucado

Compiled and adapted by Tama Fortner

Published in Nashville, Tennessee, by Tommy Nelson. Tommy Nelson is an imprint of Thomas Nelson. Thomas Nelson is a registered trademark of HarperCollins Christian Publishing, Inc.

Tommy Nelson titles may be purchased in bulk for educational, business, fund-raising, or sales promotional use. For information, please e-mail SpecialMarkets@ThomasNelson.com.

ISBN-13: 978-0-7180-1631-9

Library of Congress Cataloging-in-Publication Data is on file.

Printed in China

15 16 17 18 19 20 DSC 6 5 4 3 2 1

Mfr: DSC / Shenzhen, China / January 2015 / PO # 9321175

CONTENTS

Dear Parents . . .

In raising our girls, Denalyn and I have learned that there are many things we can do for them. We can tie their shoes so they don't trip and fall. We can make sure they have warm clothes and full tummies. We can even help them tackle some of the mysteries of higher math. But there are some things that we, as parents, simply cannot do—no matter how much we may want to or how hard we may try.

Here's what parents cannot do:

- Eliminate all scrapes and bruises.
- Banish every bully, bad-tempered teacher, or cranky friend.
- Guarantee a level playing field or a fair shake.

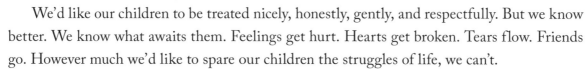

We'd like our children to be treated nicely, honestly, gently, and respectfully. But we know better. We know what awaits them. Feelings get hurt. Hearts get broken. Tears flow. Friends go. However much we'd like to spare our children the struggles of life, we can't.

But we can do this: we can teach them to pray. We can teach them to talk to God about everything, anything, any time, and all the time. We can't promise an easy life, but we can equip them to face life. We can't be with them always, but God can. So . . .

Let's teach our children to pray.

Children have a great capacity for faith. They enter the world soft-hearted, open-minded, and wide-eyed: all prerequisites for a prayerful heart. Childhood is the best window for learning prayer. Say "let's pray" to a child, and he bows his head and folds his hands. Children also have a great capacity to see the unseen and to imagine the invisible. They aren't beholden to pride, résumés, and appearances. Prayer—an act for the humble—fits the little child.

Let's teach our children to forgive and receive forgiveness.

The earlier a child can learn to both give and receive forgiveness, the more he will live a forgiven life. The prayerless child doesn't know what to do with mistakes. Prayer teaches our children to say, "I'm sorry" to God. Heaven knows they'll need this ability as adults. Prayer equips them with the dialog of grace and prepares them to be conduits of forgiveness—to themselves and to others.

Let's teach our children to hope.

Prayer sows the seeds of heaven in the heart of a child. At some point, every child will be disappointed by the troubles of this life. Let's teach them to look to the next life for hope.

Prayer—a conversation with heaven—facilitates this. The earlier our children learn that heaven is real, that it's our hometown and a wonderful place God has made for us, the less earthbound they will live, filling their lives with great purpose and a godly perspective.

Let's teach our children that God cares.

Most of all, prayer teaches our children the greatest of truths: *God listens to us!* He cares enough to incline His ear in our direction. He wants to know what we think. He even considers our opinion.

Teach your children to pray.

As you teach them everything else—piano, reading, bike-riding, and sports—teach them the one thing that they can take with them wherever they go: teach them to pray.

MAKE PRAYER TIME A PRIORITY. Don't limit your prayer time to a few seconds before bed. Eyes are too heavy and bodies too weary to make this a teachable moment. Find some prime real estate on the daily calendar and stake it off as prayer time. Give it the same emphasis you would give homework or baseball practice. Kids discern what matters by the amount of time given to it. Let them see: *prayer matters*.

MODEL PRAYER. At mealtimes and bedtimes, of course. But in good times and tough times, make prayer the go-to tool for your family. Raise them in a house where prayer is the predicted practice, not the extreme exception. Be the parent who responds to traffic jams with a prayer, not anger. Enter every activity over the threshold of prayer. As your child begins to study for the big test: "Lord, open our minds as we read," or goes out the door for the big game, "Lord, keep us alert as we play."

Let your children see you take your concerns to God. Spare them the empty, rote, and meaningless prayers. Expose them to your heartfelt requests: "God, I have too much to do; please help!"

LASTLY, TEACH YOUR CHILD THE POWER of reading and memorizing the prayers of others. Many of the ones you read in this book are time-tested, loved, and appreciated by generations. Others, like the ones we have written, are more recent. Read them all. Memorize your favorites and repeat them with your kids. By doing so you'll instill a vocabulary of faith in their hearts that will help shield them their whole lives through. May God help you teach your child to be a child of prayer.

—MAX & DENALYN

GOOD MORNING, GOD

Lord, every morning you hear my voice.
Every morning, I tell you what I need.
And I wait for your answer.

—Psalm 5:3

Blessed Jesus

Blessed Jesus, Holy One,
Thank You for this morning sun.

Blessed Jesus, full of **love**,
Look on me from high above.

Blessed Jesus, full of light,
Show me, Lord, what is **right**.

If God had a refrigerator, your picture would be on it. . . .

He sends you flowers every spring and a sunrise every morning.

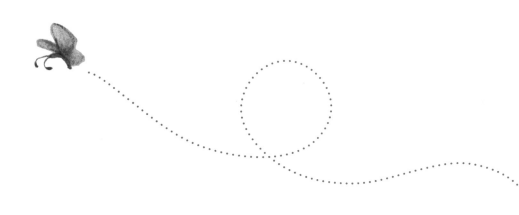

Blessed Jesus, gentle and mild,
Remember me, a little child.

Blessed Jesus, on this day,
Keep me safe, this I pray,
In Jesus' name, amen.

—MAX & DENALYN

Before I Play

Now, before I run to play,
Let me not forget to pray
To God who kept me through the night
And waked me with the morning light.

Help me, Lord, to love You more
Than I ever loved before,
In my work and in my play,
Please be with me through the day.
Amen.

—AUTHOR UNKNOWN

A New Day

Today, please make each deed of mine
    Gentle and patient, pure and kind.
Give friends to me, and work and fun,
    With love and laughter, song and sun.
Teach me to help those whom I can,
    To try to live by Your perfect plan.
Make this a day of joyful dawning,
    As full of love as this good morning.

—JOHN MARTIN, *ADAPTED*

Sing!

I will sing about your strength.
    In the morning I will sing about your love.

—PSALM 59:16

A Prayer for My Day

I thank You, Lord, for quiet rest,
And for Your watchful care of me;
Oh, let me through the day be blessed
And help me all Your gifts to see.

Oh, let me love You;
You are kind to little children such as I.
Give me a gentle, holy heart.
Lord, please be my loving Friend on high.

Help me to please my parents dear,
And to do whatever they tell;
Bless all my friends, both far and near,
And keep them ever safe and well.

—MARY L. DUNCAN, *ADAPTED*

All I Do and Say

O Lord, my God, to You I pray
While from my bed I rise.
May all I do and all I say
Be pleasing in Your eyes.
Amen.

—AUTHOR UNKNOWN

Morning Bright

The morning bright
With rosy light
Has waked me from my sleep;
Father, I know
You love me so,
With love that is so deep.

All through the day,
I humbly pray,
Please be my Guard and Guide;
My sins forgive
And let me live,
Blessed Jesus, by Your side.
Amen.

—THOMAS O. SUMMERS, *ADAPTED*

From Your Little Child

Through the night Your angels kept
Watch beside me while I slept.
Now the dark has gone away;
Thank You, Lord, for this new day.

North and South and East and West
May Your holy name be blessed;
Everywhere beneath the sun,
As in heaven, Your will be done.

Give me food that I may live;
Every naughtiness forgive;
Keep all evil things away
From Your little child this day.

—WILLIAM CANTON, *ADAPTED*

You Love Me, Jesus!

Jesus, You love me so much!

You love me when I'm grumpy,
You love me when I'm mean.
You love me morning, noon, and night,
And all times in between.

You love me when I'm happy,
You love me when I'm sad.
Because You love me all the time,
Then all the time I'm glad.

—Max & Denalyn

Happy Things

Thank You, God, for this new day,
In my school, at work and play.
Please be with me all day long,
In every story, game, and song.
May all the happy things we do
Make You, our Father, happy too.

—Author Unknown

Father, We Thank You

Father, we thank You for the night,
And for the pleasant morning light;
For rest and food and loving care,
And all that makes the day so fair.

Help us to do the things we should,
To be to others kind and good;
In all we do at work or play
To grow more loving every day.

—REBECCA J. WESTON

Joy of Morning

My Father, for another night
Of quiet sleep and rest,
For all the joy of morning light,
Your holy name be blessed.

—HENRY WILLIAM BAKER

A Morning Prayer

Our heavenly Father, it's You we praise
In this our morning prayer,
For quiet nights and happy days,
For love and tender care.

Help us in all we do and all we say
To be gentle and be good,
And always in our work and play
To do the things we should.

—Evelyn Ellis, *ADAPTED*

In the Morning

Tell me in the morning about your love.
    I trust you.
Show me what I should do
    because my prayers go up to you. . . .
Teach me to do what you want,
    because you are my God.

—Psalm 143:8, 10

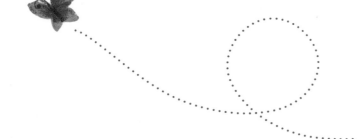

Early Morning

In the early morning,
With the sun's first rays,
All God's little children,
Give You thanks and praise.

I, too, give thanks to You,
Jesus, Shepherd dear,
For hearing my prayer,
For Your loving care.

And I would ask of You,
Be with me this day,
Never let me wander,
Close by You I'll stay. Amen.

—MARY WELDON, *ADAPTED*

When I Wake

When I wake up in the morning,
    thank You, God, for being there.
When I come to school each day,
    thank You, God, for being there.
When I am playing with my friends,
    thank You, God, for being there.
And when I go to bed at night,
    thank You, God, for being there.

—AUTHOR UNKNOWN

All for You

All for You, dear God.
Everything I do,
Or think,
Or say,
The whole day long.
Help me to be good.

—Author Unknown

Help Me, Lord

Lord,
Help me to live this day
Quietly, easily.
Help me to lean upon Your
Great strength
Trustingly, restfully,
To wait for the unfolding
Of Your will
Patiently, serenely,
To meet others
Peacefully, joyfully,
To face tomorrow
Confidently, courageously.
Amen.

—St. Francis of Assisi, *Adapted*

At the Coming of the Day

Come into my soul, Lord,
As the dawn breaks into the sky;
Let Your sun rise in my heart
At the coming of the day.

—TRADITIONAL

Every Morning

Fill us with your love every morning.
    Then we will sing and rejoice all our lives.

—PSALM 90:14

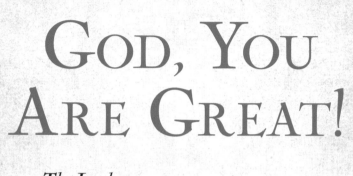

GOD, YOU ARE GREAT!

The Lord is great.

He is worthy of our praise.

No one can understand how great he is.

—PSALM 145:3

God Is So Good!

God, You are so good.

You made singing birds.

You made puffy clouds.

You made blue skies and

tall, tall mountains.

And You even made me!

Thanks for everything You made.

What is praise? Praise is telling the Lord how great He is.

God, You are so good.

You love everybody!

Big people, small people, tall people,

and short people.

You love all people.

You even love me!

I love you, God. You are so good!

—MAX & DENALYN

God Made All Things

God, You made all things;
  the sun to rule the day, the moon to shine by night.
You made the great whale, and the elephant,
  and the worm that crawls upon the ground.
The little birds sing praise to You;
  the brooks and rivers praise You too.
I will praise You with my voice,
  Though I am a little child.
  And I will love You all my life.

—ANNA LAETITIA BARBAULD, *ADAPTED*

From God's Hand

You made this world so broad and grand,
And filled it with blessings from Your hand.
You made the sky so big and blue,
And all the little children, too.

—AUTHOR UNKNOWN

This Earth of Ours

The beautiful bright sunshine

That smiles on all below,

The waving trees, the cool, soft breeze,

The rippling streams that flow,

The shadows on the hillsides,

The many tinted flowers,

With greatest love and tender care

You made this earth of ours.

—AUTHOR UNKNOWN

With All My Heart

I will praise you, Lord, with all my heart.

I will tell all the miracles you have done.

I will be happy because of you.

God Most High, I will sing praises

to your name.

—PSALM 9:1–2

29

God of Miracles

Dear God,

You are a God of miracles,
Some I see and some I don't.

You make a flower bloom
From a tiny seed in dirt.
You make my heart be kind
When I'd really like to hurt.

You made the oceans salty,
The sky so bright and clean.
And, God, You help me to forgive
When a friend is being mean.

You are a God of miracles
And some I understand.
You love creating beauty
In hearts and on the land.

—MAX & DENALYN

I Will Sing!

I myself will sing to the Lord.
> I will make music to the Lord,
> the God of Israel.

—JUDGES 5:3

Praise God

Praise God from whom all blessings flow;
Praise Him, all creatures here below;
Praise Him above, ye heavenly host;
Praise Father, Son, and Holy Ghost.

—BISHOP THOMAS KEN, *ADAPTED*

God of All

O God, You are the God of all,
The God of heaven and earth,
Of the sea and the rivers;
The God of the sun and of the moon and of all the stars;
The God of the lofty mountains and of the lowly valleys,
You live in the heavens, and the earth, and the sea,
    and in everything that is in them.

—St. Patrick

Day and Night

Both the day and the night are yours.
    You made the sun and the moon.
You made all the limits on the earth.
    You created summer and winter.

—Psalm 74:16–17

The Maker

He only is the Maker
Of all things near and far;
He paints the wayside flower,
He lights the evening star;
The winds and waves obey Him,
By Him the birds are fed;
Much more to us, His children,
He gives our daily bread.
All good gifts around us
Are sent from heaven above;
Then thank the Lord,
O thank the Lord
For all His love.

—MATTHIAS CLAUDIUS, *ADAPTED*

The Lord Is Great

I will praise you every day.
I will praise you forever and ever.
The Lord is great. He is worthy of our praise.
No one can understand how great he is.

—PSALM 145:2–3

Big and Great!

God, You are big,
God, You are great.
You know all that I feel.
You know all that I think.

You know when I'm happy.
And You know when I'm hurt.
When I'm happy, You're happy.
And when I hurt, You hurt.

You make me smile when I'm sad,
And You wipe my tears away.
You do all these things, God,
Because You are big and great.

—MAX & DENALYN

My God

Lord, you are my God.
    I honor you and praise you.
You have done amazing things.
    You have always done what you said you would.

—ISAIAH 25:1

Great God

Great God, I know You listen,
For You are my Father and my Friend.
Though I am little and You are so high,
Lord of all the earth, air, and sky.

—Ann Taylor Gilbert, *adapted*

God, My Father

Dear God, You are wise and loving,
You are great and strong;
Happy when we do right,
And sad when we do wrong.

Dear God, my Father,
Guide me every hour;
Keep me safe and shield me
With Your holy power. Amen.

—Traditional

Lord, You Are . . .

You are holy, Lord, the only God,
And Your ways are wonderful.
You are strong.
You are great.
You are the Most High,
You are almighty.
You, holy Father, are
King of heaven and earth.
You are love.
You are wisdom.
You are strength.
You are rest.
You are peace.
You are joy and gladness.
You are fair and just to all.
You are beauty.
You are gentleness.
You protect us.
You guard and defend us.
You are courage.
You are our safety and our hope.
You are our faith,
Our great comfort.
You are our eternal life,
Great and wonderful Lord,
God almighty,
Merciful Savior.

—St. Francis of Assisi, *ADAPTED*

It Is Good

It is good to praise the Lord,
    to sing praises to God Most High.
It is good to tell of your love in the morning
    and of your loyalty at night. . . .
Lord, you have made me happy by what you have done.

—PSALM 92:1–2, 4

For the Beauty of the Earth

For the beauty of the earth,
For the beauty of the skies,
For the love which from our birth,
Over and around us lies,
Lord of all, to You we raise
This our hymn of grateful praise.

For the beauty of each hour
Of the day and of the night,
Hill and vale, and tree and flower,
Sun and moon, and stars of light,
Lord of all, to You we raise
This our hymn of grateful praise.

—FOLLIOTT S. PIERPOINT, *ADAPTED*

The Most Wonderful Name

Lord our Master,
 your name is the most wonderful name in all the earth! . . .
I look at the heavens,
 which you made with your hands.
I see the moon and stars,
 which you created. . . .
Lord our Master,
 your name is the most wonderful name in all the earth!

—PSALM 8:1, 3, 9

Holy Lord

Lord, Your glory fills the heaven,
And covers the earth below;
Unto You is glory given,
Holy, holy, holy Lord.

—BISHOP R. MANT, *ADAPTED*

The Heavens

The heavens tell the glory of God.
And the skies announce what his hands have made.

—PSALM 19:1

You Are My God

You made the earth and all the clouds!
    You are awesome, God!
You made the oceans and built the beaches!
    You are great, God!
You made the giraffe's tall neck, the elephant's long
        trunk, and the lion's loud roar!
    You are amazing, God!
The stars twinkle, the rivers run, and the birds sing—
        all because of You.
    I am so glad You are my God!

—Max & Denalyn

God Is Worthy

Our Lord and God! You are worthy
    to receive glory and honor and power.
You made all things.
    Everything existed and was made
    because you wanted it.

—Revelation 4:11

Lord Most High

All things praise You, Lord most high!
Heaven and earth and sea and sky!
All were for Your glory made,
That Your greatness would be displayed.

—GEORGE WILLIAM CONDER, *ADAPTED*

Sing to the Lord

My whole being, praise the Lord.
    Lord my God, you are very great.
You are clothed with glory and majesty.
    You wear light like a robe.
    You stretch out the skies like a tent.
    You build your room above the clouds.
You make the clouds your chariot.
    You ride on the wings of the wind. . . .
I will sing to the Lord all my life.
    I will sing praises to my God as long as I live.

—PSALM 104:1–3, 33

My Family and Friends

The Father has loved us so much!
He loved us so much that we are called children of God.

—1 John 3:1

How do you think Jesus treated His family? With kindness and patience, with love and respect.

God Cares About Me and All I See

Thank You, God for:

Sisters and brothers,
Moms and dads,
Grandmas and grandpas,
Uncles and aunts.

For bees and trees,
For rain and snow,
Grass that's green,
And winds that blow.

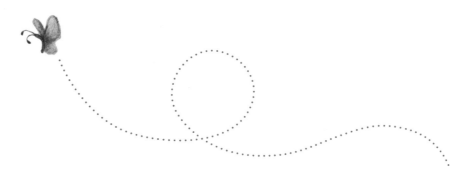

For my best friend
Who lives close by,
For hide-and-seek
And apple pie.

Thank You, God, for lots of everything:

Running and swimming,
Writing and reading,
Jumping and dancing,
Skipping and singing.

For rabbits and cats,
Horses and dogs,
Cows and pigs,
And ants on a log.

There's so much more to thank You for . . .
So I'll just say, I love You, Lord!

—MAX & DENALYN

Bless All

God bless all those that I love,
God bless all those that love me;
And bless all those that love those
      that I love,
And all those that love those that love me.

—FROM AN OLD NEW ENGLAND SAMPLER

46

Look Down from Above

Dear Father in heaven,
Look down from above;
Bless Father and Mother
And all whom I love.

—Traditional

Friend of Little Children

Jesus, friend of little children,
Be a friend to me;
Take my hand and ever keep me
Close to Thee.

Never leave me nor desert me,
Always be my friend;
For I need You, from life's beginning
To its end.

—Walter John Mathams, *Adapted*

God Our Father

May the love of God our Father
    Be in all our homes today;
May the love of the Lord Jesus
    Keep our hearts and minds always;
May His loving Holy Spirit
    Guide and bless the ones I love,
Father, mother, brothers, sisters,
    Keep them safely in His love.

—AUTHOR UNKNOWN

Parents and Children

Bless all parents in their children,
    And all children in their parents.

—CHRISTINA ROSSETTI

The Builder

Unless the LORD builds the house,
    the builders labor in vain.

—PSALM 127:1 NIV

All Who Love Me

Bless, O Lord Jesus, my parents,
    And all who love me and take care of me.

Make me loving to them,
    Polite and obedient, helpful and kind.

—AUTHOR UNKNOWN

Father, Help Me

Father, help me to obey my parents,
Because that is the right thing to do.
Amen.

—BASED ON EPHESIANS 6:1

For Our Homes

Thank You, Father, for our homes,
For our parents kind and true,
Most of all for Your dear Son,
May we try His will to do.
Amen.

—Author Unknown

No One Like the Lord

There is no one holy like the Lord.
There is no God but you.
There is no Rock like our God.

—1 Samuel 2:2

Hear My Prayer

Heavenly Father, hear my prayer;
   Night and day I'm in Your care;
Look upon me from above,
   Bless the home I dearly love;
Bless the friends with whom I play,
   Make us kinder day by day.

—Author Unknown

For Happy Hearts

We thank You, Lord, for happy hearts,
For rain and sunny weather.
Thank You, Father, for this food
And that we are together.

—Traditional

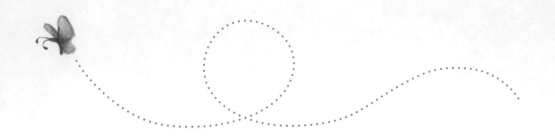

Our Family

Lord, look down on our family gathered here.
We thank You for this place in which we live,
    for the love that unites us,
    for the peace given to us this day,
    for the hope with which we look to tomorrow;
for the health, the work, the food, and the bright skies,
    that make our lives delightful;
    for our friends in all parts of the earth. Amen.

—ROBERT LOUIS STEVENSON, *ADAPTED*

Family, Friends, and Neighbors

Thank You, Lord, for giving me
    A happy, caring family.
Thank You for the friends I meet;
    And for neighbors down the street.
But most of all, dear Lord above,
    I thank You for Your precious love.

—TRADITIONAL

For Friends

Thank You for my friend next door,
And my friend across the street,
And please help me to be a friend
To everyone I meet.

—Author Unknown

As You Love Me

Lord, teach me to love my family and friends,
Just as You love me.
In Jesus' name, amen.

—based on John 15:12

Our House

Our house has big windows
So the sun can shine bright.

Our house has warm beds
To sleep in at night.

Our house has a door
For all of our friends.

Our house has four walls
To keep out the winds.

Our house has everything!
And I'm thankful to You.

Because, dear God,
You live here too.

—MAX & DENALYN

Bless My Home

O dear God, love this home of mine,
And all who live within,
Care for our bodies, bless our hearts,
And keep our lives from sin.
God, make my home a house of joy,
Where love and faith are given,
Make it the dearest place to You:
The nearest place to heaven. Amen.

—JOHN MARTIN

In Your Loving Care

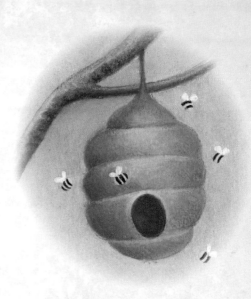

Dear Lord, I'd like to pray
    for all the people that I love,
    but who live far away.
Tonight with them my thoughts I share.
Please keep them in Your loving care,
    each night and every day.

—Traditional

Bless and Keep

May the Lord bless you and keep you.
May the Lord show his kindness.
May he have mercy on you.
May the Lord watch over you and give you peace.

—Numbers 6:24–26

The Robin's Song

God bless the field and bless the furrow,
Stream and branch and rabbit burrow,
Hill and stone and flower and tree,
Bless the lane and bless the street,
Bless the minnow, bless the whale,
Bless the rainbow and the hail,
Bless the nest and bless the leaf,
Bless the righteous and the thief,
Bless the wing and bless the fin,
Bless the air I travel in,
Bless the mill and bless the mouse,
Bless the baker and his house,
Bless the earth and bless the sea,
God bless you and God bless me!

—RICHARD HONEYWOOD, *ADAPTED*

All Things Everywhere

For friends and grass and trees,
We thank You, Lord above.
For smiling flowers and earth,
And sunny skies above.

We know Your tender love.
We thank You for Your care,
For light, and fields, and flowers,
And all things everywhere. Amen.

—AUTHOR UNKNOWN

All Things Great and Small

He prays best, who loves best
All things both great and small;
For the dear God who loves us,
He made and loves us all.

—SAMUEL TAYLOR COLERIDGE, *ADAPTED*

57

In My Play and Through My Day

There is a right time for everything . . .
a time to laugh . . .
a time to dance . . .
a time to hug . . .
a time to love.

—Ecclesiastes 3:1, 4, 5, 8

Play

This is the day I get to **play**.

Watch me, God, along the way.

When I run as fast as I can,

Or **build** a castle in the sand,

You can talk to God because
God listens. Always. . . . .

He listens in the
morning and in the night.

While on a swing and flying high,
Or chasing the yellow butterfly.
This day will be the best of all.
Jumping, skipping, throwing a ball.
Keep me safe. Watch over me and then . . .
Tomorrow, dear God, can I play again?

—MAX & DENALYN

61

A Fine, Good Day

Today I'll have some things to do.

O may I do my very best.

Help me to think of others, too,

When I would rather play or rest.

O God, please let me have some fun;

Please love me when I work or play,

So when night comes, and day is done,

I'll know I've had a fine, good day.

—John Martin

Be with Me Today

Lord Jesus Christ,
Be with me today,
And help me
In all I think, or do, or say.

—TRADITIONAL

God's Children

You are God's children whom he loves.
So try to be like God. Live a life of love.
Love other people just as Christ loved us.

—EPHESIANS 5:1–2

A Little Light

God, make my life a little light
Within the world to glow;
A little flame that burns so bright
Wherever I may go.

God, make my life a little flower
That gives sweet joy to all,
Happy to bloom, by Your great power
Although I may be small.

God, make my life a little song
To give comfort to the sad,
That helps others to be strong
And makes the singer glad.

God, make my life a little staff
On which the weak may rest,
And with what health and strength I have
May I serve my neighbors best.

God, make my life a little hymn
Of tenderness and praise;
Of faith, that never fades or dims,
In all Your wondrous ways.

—Matilda Betham-Edwards, *adapted*

Working for the Lord

In all the work you are doing,
    work the best you can.
Work as if you were working for the Lord,
    not for men.

—Colossians 3:23

On This Day

Loving Father, on this day
Make us happy in our play,
Kind and helpful, playing fair,
Letting others have a share.

—Author Unknown

A Busy Day

Lord, You know how busy I must be this day.
If I forget You, please do not forget me.

—Sir Jacob Astley

Your Throne on High

Jesus, from Your throne on high,
　　Far above the bright blue sky,
Look on me with loving eye;
　　Hear me, Holy Jesus.

Please be with me every day,
　　In my work and in my play,
When I learn and when I pray;
　　Hear me, Holy Jesus.

—Thomas B. Pollock, *Adapted*

God's Great Love

Is it so small a thing
To have enjoyed the sun,
To have lived light in the spring,
To have loved, to have thought, to have done?
O thank You, heavenly Father, for Your great love!

—MATTHEW ARNOLD

This Is the Day

This is the day that the Lord has made.
Let us rejoice and be glad today!

—PSALM 118:24

I Saw . . .

God,

I saw You today while I was at play!

I saw Your creation throughout the day.

I saw a flock of birds fly high in the sky.

I saw the golden wings on a butterfly.

I saw a puppy, furry and small.

I saw a tree, so strong and so tall.

I saw the sun and thought of Your light.

I saw the moon shine bright at night.

I saw the rainbow after the rain.

I saw the farm with its grass and grain.

Thank You for making everything I see.

Most of all, God, thanks for making me!

—Max & Denalyn

More Like You, Lord

Lord of the loving heart, may mine be loving too.

Lord of the gentle hands, may mine be gentle too.

Lord of the willing feet, may mine be willing too.

So I may grow more like You

In all I say and do.

—Author Unknown

Through This Day

Lord, through this day,
   In work and play,
     Please bless each thing I do.
May I be honest, loving, kind,
   Obedient unto You.

—Author Unknown

Today

Dear Lord Jesus,
We shall have this day only once;
   Before it is gone,
     Help us to do all the good we can,
So that today is not a wasted day.

—Stephen Grellet

To Do Good

We must not become tired of doing good.

—Galatians 6:9

From A to Z!

Thank You, God, for making me
just as I am from A to Z.

Alive,
Breathing,
Caring,
Daring,
Excited,
Fun,
Great,
Happy,
Important,
Joyful,
Kind,
Loving,
Marvelous,
Noisy,
Older,
Patient,
Quiet,
Rambunctious,
Silly,
Thankful,
Useful,
Vibrant,
Wiggly,
eXtra special,
Yours, and

Zippity-zesty!

—Max & Denalyn

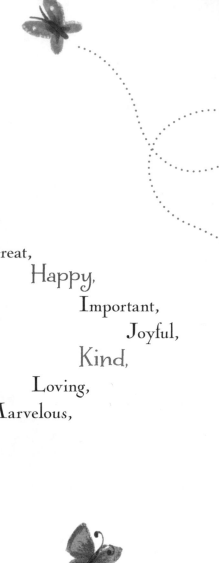

Amazing and Wonderful

Dear Lord,
You made my whole being.

You formed me in my mother's body.

I praise you because you made me in an amazing and wonderful way.

What you have done is wonderful.

I know this very well.

—Psalm 139:13–14

My Words

Keep my little tongue today,
Keep it gentle while I play.
Keep my hands from doing wrong.
Keep my feet the whole day long;
Keep me all, O Jesus mild,
Keep me ever Your dear child. Amen.

—Unknown

The Lord, My Rock

I hope my words and thoughts please you.

Lord, you are my Rock, the one who saves me.

—Psalm 19:14

This Day

Lord, be with me this day.

    Within me . . .

    Above me . . .

    Beneath me . . .

    Before me . . .

    Behind me . . .

    Around me.

—BASED UPON A PRAYER BY St. Patrick

Hear My Prayer

Father in heaven hear my prayer,

Keep me in Thy loving care.

Be my guide in all I do,

Bless all those who love me too.

Amen.

—Author Unknown

Jesus, Keep Me

Jesus, keep me every day,

When I work and when I play,

When I think and when I talk,

When I run and when I walk.

Keep me, Jesus, this I pray,

Lead me, keep me, every day.

—John O. Foster

For Happy Days

Thank You for each happy day,
For fun, for friends, and work and play;
Thank You for Your loving care,
Here at home and everywhere.

—AUTHOR UNKNOWN

God in Heaven

Thank You, God in heaven,
For a day begun.
Thank You for the breezes,
Thank You for the sun.

For this time of gladness,
For our work and play,
Thank You, God in heaven,
For another day.

—TRADITIONAL

MY MEALTIME PRAYERS

So if you eat, or if you drink, or if you do anything, do everything for the glory of God.

—1 CORINTHIANS 10:31

One of the sweetest reasons God saves you is because He likes you. . . .

So Yummy!

Thank You for the food we eat.
It's very good and very sweet.

Thank You, God. It fills my tummy.
All this food—it is so yummy.

Thank You, God. You fill my plate.
Thank You, God. You are great!

—MAX & DENALYN

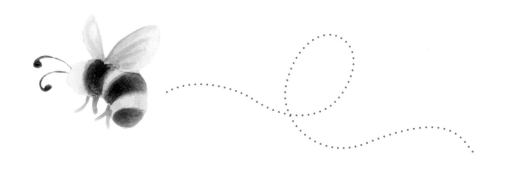

He thinks you are the best thing to come along since peanut butter!

The World So Sweet

Thank You for the world so sweet,
Thank You for the food we eat,
Thank You for the birds that sing,
Thank You, God, for everything!

—Edith Rutter Leatham

Good Gifts

For rosy apples, juicy plums
And honey from the bees,
We thank You, heavenly Father God,
For such good gifts as these.

—Author Unknown

We Give Thanks

With every bite we eat,
Let us not forget to give thanks.
Whatever brings us Your blessing shall be
To the glory of Your name.
We give thanks to You because You are kind
And Your goodness will last forever.
So let us give thanks to You our Lord,
And give You the praise for all the gifts
Which You have given to us.

—LUDWIG HELMBOLD, *ADAPTED*

Folded Hands

Our hands we fold,
And heads we bow,
For food and drink
We ask Thee now.
Amen.

—AUTHOR UNKNOWN

God Gives to All

He gives food to every living creature.

His love continues forever.

—Psalm 136:25

The Good Seed

We plough the fields and scatter
The good seed on the land,
But it is fed and watered
By God's almighty hand;
He sends the snow in winter,
The warmth to swell the grain,
The breezes and the sunshine,
And soft refreshing rain.
All good gifts around us
Are sent from heaven above;
Then thank the Lord,
O thank the Lord
For all His love.

—Matthias Claudius, *adapted*

Much More Than Birds

Look at the birds in the air.

They don't plant or harvest or store food in barns.

But your heavenly Father feeds the birds.

And you know that you are worth much more than the birds.

—Matthew 6:26

Truly Thankful

For what we are about to receive,
May the Lord make us truly thankful.
Amen.

—Traditional

Our Daily Bread

Give us this day our daily bread;
Our table is so beautifully spread,
Show us how best to save with care,
Until our every loaf we share
With hungry children everywhere.
Father, that all be fed,
Give us our daily bread.

—Alice E. Allen, *adapted*

We Praise

For health and strength and daily food,
we praise Your name, O Lord.

—Traditional

Bless Us All Our Days

For these and all Your gifts of love
    We give You thanks and praise;
Look down, O Father, from above
    And bless us all our days.
We thank You, God, for this good food
    That You have given today;
And help us all grow strong and good,
    To live for You, we pray.

—AUTHOR UNKNOWN

Every Little Thing

God,
You know and love every little thing about me—
From my name to the number of hairs on my head.
You give me food for eating and clothes for wearing.
You give me everything I need.
    When I am happy, You care,
    When I fall down, You care,
    When I feel afraid, You care,
Because You know and love every little thing about me.

—MAX & DENALYN

Praise the Lord!

Lord,

The earth is full of the things you made.

You make the grass for cattle

   and vegetables for the use of man.

    You make the food grown from the earth. . . .

My whole being, praise the Lord.

Praise the Lord.

—PSALM 104:13–14, 35

Bless This Food

Be present at our table, Lord;
Be here and everywhere adored.
Bless this food and all that we do,
So one day we may feast with You.
Amen.

—JOHN CENNICK, *ADAPTED*

To Serve You, Lord

Bless me, O Lord, and let this food
Make me stronger to serve You,
For Jesus Christ's sake. Amen.

—ISAAC WATTS, *ADAPTED*

Our Holy Guest

Come, Lord Jesus, be our Guest;
And may our meal by You be blessed.

—MARTIN LUTHER, *ADAPTED*

By His Hand

God is great, and God is good.
Let us thank Him for our food.
By His hand we all are fed;
Thank You, Lord, for our bread.

—Traditional

For Food and Friends

For food to eat
    and those who prepare it;
For health to enjoy it
    and friends to share it;
Thank You, Heavenly Father.
Amen.

—Traditional

GOD TAKES CARE OF ME

The Lord is all I need.
He takes care of me.

—Psalm 16:5

God Has Blessed Me

Daddy God,

You have blessed me, Lord, with so many things.

You give me Your love and make my heart sing.

You give me Your joy so I can have fun.

You give me Your kindness, bright as the sun.

Faith is believing that God
will do what is right.

You teach me patience so I can love well.

You fill me with peace so others can tell

That Jesus is love and lives in my heart.

You hold me close so we're never apart.

—Max & Denalyn

God loves and blesses me . . .

Hear and Bless

Dear Father, hear and bless
Your beasts and singing birds:
And guard with tenderness
Small things that have no words.

—Author Unknown

So Great a Love

For God loved the world
    so much that he gave his only Son.
God gave his Son so that whoever
    believes in him may not be lost,
    but have eternal life.

—John 3:16

Call to the Lord

The Lord is my rock, my place of safety, my Savior.
My God is my rock.
    I can run to him for safety.
He is my shield and my saving strength.
    The Lord is my high tower and my place of safety. . . .
I will call to the Lord.

—2 Samuel 22:3–4

When I need help . . .

God, My Friend

Would You help me?

   When I bump my head, would You heal it?

   If my throat aches, would You help it?

   Sometimes my tummy hurts, would You help me feel better?

Please help me.

When I feel sad, please help me smile.

When I am afraid, please be my friend.

—MAX & DENALYN

God, Who Loves Me

You are my protection,

   my place of safety in times of trouble.

God, my strength, I will sing praises to you.

   God, my protection, you are the God who loves me.

—PSALM 59:16–17

The Twenty-Third Psalm

The Lord is my shepherd.

    I have everything I need.

He gives me rest in green pastures.

    He leads me to calm water.

He gives me new strength.

For the good of his name,

    he leads me on paths that are right.

Even if I walk

    through a very dark valley,

I will not be afraid

    because you are with me.

Your rod and your walking stick comfort me.

You prepare a meal for me

    in front of my enemies.

You pour oil on my head.

    You give me more than I can hold.

Surely your goodness and love will be with me

    all my life.

And I will live in the house of the Lord forever.

—PSALM 23

When I am afraid . . .

Shoo!

Thunderstorms are big and loud,
Especially in the night,
When thunder makes a boom
And lightning makes the light.

Sometimes I am afraid
And I don't know what to do.
I pray to You, sweet Jesus,
And You tell my fears to "Shoo!"

—Max & Denalyn

Trusting God

When I am afraid,
I will trust you.

—Psalm 56:3

Under His Wings

He will protect you like a bird
   spreading its wings over its young.

—Psalm 91:4

Loving Shepherd

Loving Shepherd of Your sheep,
Hold me safely while I sleep.
Nothing can against You stand;
You keep me safe in Your hand.

We would praise You every day,
Gladly all Your will obey,
Like Your blessed ones above
Happy in Your precious love.

Loving Shepherd, ever near,
Teach Your lambs Your voice to hear;
Suffer not our steps to stray
From the straight and narrow way.

—JANE E. LEESON, *ADAPTED*

The Weather

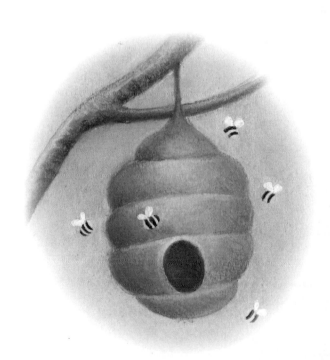

When the weather is wet,
    We must not fret.
When the weather is dry,
    We must not cry.
When the weather is warm,
    We must not storm.
When the weather is cold,
    We must not scold.
Be thankful together,
    Whatever the weather.

—AUTHOR UNKNOWN

When I am feeling all alone . . .

Wherever I Go

There is no place where You are not—
Wherever I go, there You are.
Now and always You uphold me with Your power
And keep me safe in Your love.

—AUTHOR UNKNOWN

Strong and Brave

Be strong and brave. . . .
Don't be frightened.
The Lord your God will go with you.
He will not leave you or forget you.

—DEUTERONOMY 31:6

Little Jesus

Little Jesus, were You shy
Once and just so small as I?
And what did it feel like to be
Out of heaven, and just like me?

—FRANCIS THOMPSON, *ADAPTED*

God Loves Us All

God, You made the birds and flowers
    And all things large and small;
You'll not forget Your little ones;
    I know You love us all.

—AUTHOR UNKNOWN

You Know Me, Lord

Lord, you have examined me.
    You know all about me.
You know when I sit down and when I get up.
    You know my thoughts before I think them.
You know where I go and where I lie down.
    You know well everything I do.
Lord, even before I say a word,
    you already know what I am going to say.
You are all around me.

—PSALM 139:1–6

TEACH ME, GOD

Trust the Lord with all your heart.
Don't depend on your own understanding.

PROVERBS 3:5

Tell God all about your messes.
Your sins. Your mistakes.
He can fix them—and He won't
even need a Band-Aid.

Father God, Holy Spirit, and Jesus the Son

Father, You are on **earth** and in heaven today.

Jesus, You are truth; please show me Your way.

Holy Spirit, Comforter, You teach me each day

To stay close to You so I'll know how to **pray**.

—Max & Denalyn

Kind and Good

Help us to do the things we should,
To be to others kind and good,
In all we do, in all we say,
To grow more loving every day.

—REBECCA J. WESTON

All I Should Know

Lord, teach me all that I should know;
In grace and wisdom may I grow;
The more I learn to do Your will,
The better I may love You still.

—Isaac Watts, *ADAPTED*

Teach Me

Teach me, my God, my Savior.
I trust you all day long.

—Psalm 25:5

Growing More Like Jesus

Jesus, help my eyes to see
    All the good You send to me.
Jesus, help my ears to hear
    Calls for help from far and near.
Jesus, help my feet to go
    In the way that You would show.
Jesus, help my hands to do
    All things loving, kind, and true.
Jesus, may I helpful be,
    Growing every day like Thee. Amen.

—AUTHOR UNKNOWN

How to Pray

Lord, teach me what I need,
And teach me how to pray,
And do not let me seek Your face
And not mean what I say.

—JOHN BURTON, *ADAPTED*

God's Ways

Lord, tell me your ways.
Show me how to live.

—PSALM 25:4

This Little Child

Father, help this little child,
Make me truthful, good, and mild,
Kind, obedient, modest, meek,
Mindful of the words I speak.

Help me what is right to choose,
What is wrong refuse to do.
From all evil help me run,
This I ask for everyone.
Amen.

—AUTHOR UNKNOWN

A Pure Heart

Create in me a pure heart, God.
Make my spirit right again.

—Psalm 51:10

Sweet Lessons

Savior, teach me day by day
Love's sweet lesson to obey;
Sweeter lesson there cannot be,
Than loving Him who first loved me.

Teach me I am not my own,
I am Yours and Yours alone;
Yours to keep, to rule, to save,
To free from sin by Your grace.

—Jane E. Leeson, *adapted*

An Instrument of Peace

Lord, make me an instrument of Your peace;
Where there is hatred, let me sow love;
Where there is injury, pardon;
Where there is error, truth;
Where there is doubt, faith;
Where there is despair, hope;
Where there is darkness, light;
Where there is sadness, joy.

—*ATTRIBUTED TO* St. Francis of Assisi

In My Heart

God be in my head and in my understanding.
God be in mine eyes and in my looking.
God be in my mouth and in my speaking.
God be in my heart and in my understanding.

—Old Sarum Primer

Sometimes

Sometimes I mess up.
I say mean words.
I disobey my parents.
I get mad and walk away.
I am sorry.
Please forgive me.

—MAX & DENALYN

A Lie

Dear God, I told a lie today;
    I thought it was an easy way
To hide the thing that I had done
    From my parents and everyone.
Deep in my heart—far out of sight,
    I buried truth and love and right.
O God, forgive me, and I'll try
    Never to tell another lie.

—JOHN MARTIN, *ADAPTED*

Father of Us All

Dear Father of us all,
    To You our thanks we give,
Because You love every child
    Wherever he may live.
O Giver of all gifts,
    We want to be like You;
Help us to live unselfishly,
    And be kind and friendly too.

—EDITH LOVELL THOMAS, *ADAPTED*

I'm Sorry

Jesus, I'm sorry for how I acted today.

I wasn't nice.

I don't want to hurt anyone.

I don't want to be selfish.

I want to love everyone.

I want to be kind.

But, I wasn't.

Take this bad feeling from me.

With Your help, I will do better.

Thank You, Jesus. Amen.

—MAX & DENALYN

Lord, Teach Us

Lord, please teach us how to pray.

—LUKE 11:1

Teach a Little Child

Lord, teach a little child to pray,
And then accept my prayer.
You hear all the words I say
For You are everywhere.

A little sparrow cannot fall
That You, Lord, do not see,
And though I am so young and small
You take good care of me.

Teach me to do the thing that's right,
And when I sin, forgive;
And make it still my great delight
To serve You while I live.

—JANE TAYLOR, *ADAPTED*

The Love of Jesus

I ask the Father in his great glory
    to give you the power to be strong in spirit.
He will give you that strength through his Spirit.
I pray that Christ will live in your hearts
    because of your faith.
I pray that your life will be strong in love
    and be built on love.
And I pray that you and all God's holy people
    will have the power to understand
    the greatness of Christ's love.
I pray that you can understand how wide and how long
    and how high and how deep that love is.
Christ's love is greater than any person can ever know.
But I pray that you will be able to know that love.
Then you can be filled with the fullness of God.

—EPHESIANS 3:16–19

Dear Lord . . .

Please give me what I ask, dear Lord,
If you'd be glad about it.
But if you think it's not for me,
Please help me do without it.

—Anonymous

PRAYERS FOR SPECIAL DAYS

Rejoice in the Lord always.
I will say it again: Rejoice!

PHILIPPIANS 4:4 NIV

What will it be like to finally see Jesus face-to-face?

Happy New Year!

Jesus, You make all things new.
Every day and New Year too!
As we start a brand-new year,
Keep us safe and give us cheer.
Keep our eyes on heaven above,
Covered in Your gracious love.

—MAX & DENALYN

I imagine it will be better than Christmas morning, better than a birthday, better than an ice cream sundae—all rolled into one!

A New Year's Prayer

O Lord Christ, our Savior dear,
Please be ever near us;
Grant us now a glad New Year.
Amen, Jesus, hear us!

—AUTHOR UNKNOWN

A Winter's Prayer

It's winter now and the fallen snow
Has left the heavens all cold and clear;
Through leafless trees the sharp winds blow,
And all the earth lies dead and drear.

And yet God's love is not withdrawn;
His life within the cool air breathes,
His beauty paints the golden dawn,
And clothes the trees with icy wreaths.

O God, who gives the winter's cold
As well as summer's happy rays,
Shelter us; in Your love enfold
And keep us through life's wintry days.

—SAMUEL LONGFELLOW, *ADAPTED*

Whiter Than Snow

Take away my sin, and I will be clean.
   Wash me, and I will be whiter than snow.

—PSALM 51:7

A Springtime Prayer

Dear God in Paradise
Look upon our sowing:
Bless the little gardens
And the green things growing.

—AUTHOR UNKNOWN

Hallelujah: An Easter Prayer

Hallelujah! Hallelujah!
Jesus is alive.
Hosanna in the highest!
You make me feel alive!
I praise You with my drum.
   (Pretend you are beating a drum.)
I praise You with my tongue.
I praise You with my flute.
I praise You with my horn.
Hosanna in the highest!
We'll sing all day long.
Hallelujah! Hallelujah!
In our hearts, You put this song.

—MAX & DENALYN

Jesus Has Risen!

Let us all with joyful voice
Praise the God of heaven,
And with all our hearts rejoice,
For Jesus Christ has risen!

—Author Unknown

To Save Us All

There is a green hill far away
Outside a city wall
Where the dear Lord was crucified
Who died to save us all.

—Mrs. C. F. Alexander

A Summer Prayer

We thank You, O our Father,
    For all Your loving care;
We thank You that You have made
    The world so bright and fair.
We thank You for summer sun,
    And for the pleasant showers;
And, O our God, we thank You,
    We thank You for the flowers.

And whether in the city
    Or in the fields they dwell;
Always the same sweet message
    The fair, sweet flowers tell,
For they are all so wonderful,
    Their lovely scent leaves us awed;
And they are all so beautiful,
    They tell of Your love, O God.

—Author Unknown

God's People

Then my people, who are called by my name,
    will be sorry for what they have done.
They will pray and obey me and stop their evil ways.
If they do, I will hear them from heaven.
I will forgive their sin, and I will heal their land.

—2 Chronicles 7:14

A Fourth of July Prayer

Our fathers' God, to Thee,
Author of liberty,
To Thee we sing;
Long may our land be bright
With freedom's holy light;
Protect us by Thy might,
Great God, our King. Amen.

—Samuel F. Smith

A School Day Prayer

God bless my parents and my teachers, too;

My playmates, that I love, who are so true.

Each day I pray that I may grow to be

My Jesus' Spirit in love, pure and free.

—Author Unknown

For My Teachers

For teachers kind,

And parents dear,

For Heaven's gifts

And heart's good cheer;

For hope of bliss

In endless living,

I offer to the Lord

Thanksgiving.

—Author Unknown

A Harvest Prayer

We thank You, then, O Father,
For all things bright and good,
The seed-time and the harvest,
Our life, our health, our food;
No gifts have we to offer
For all Your love imparts,
But that which You desire,
Our humble, thankful hearts.
All good gifts around us
Are sent from heaven above;
Then thank the Lord,
O thank the Lord
For all His love.
Amen.

—MATTHIAS CLAUDIUS, *ADAPTED*

Giving Thanks

Shout to the Lord, all the earth.
Serve the Lord with joy.
Come before him with singing.
Know that the Lord is God.
He made us, and we belong to him. . . .
Thank him, and praise his name.
The Lord is good. His love continues forever.

—PSALM 100

126

A Thanksgiving Prayer

The God of harvest praise:
In loud thanksgiving raise
    Hand, heart, and voice.
The valleys laugh and sing,
Forest and mountains ring,
The plains their tribute bring;
The streams rejoice.

—Author Unknown

Shout with Joy

Shout with joy to the Lord, all the earth. . . .
Let the sea and everything in it shout.
    Let the world and everyone on it sing.
Let the rivers clap their hands.
    Let the mountains sing together for joy.
Let them sing before the Lord.

—Psalm 98:4, 7–9

Prayers at Christmastime

Happy Birthday, Jesus.

You once were little, just like me.

A baby in a crib,

With tiny hands and little feet.

You learned to walk.

You learned to talk.

You grew.

I did, too.

Sometimes I get cold; did You?

I get tired; did You, too?

Did You feel then what I feel now?

Yes, You did.

Thank You, Jesus.

You became just like me.

Now, I want to grow to be just like You.

—MAX & DENALYN

Babe of Bethlehem

Precious Babe of Bethlehem,

Gift of love to sinful men,

You are our Savior, Lord, and King—

May we all Your praises sing! Amen.

—UNKNOWN

Christmas

May Christmas morning make us happy to be Your children
And Christmas evening bring us to our beds with grateful thoughts,
Forgiving and forgiven
For Jesus' sake, amen.

—UNKNOWN

Tiny Tim's Prayer

God bless us every one!

—CHARLES DICKENS

O Little Town of Bethlehem

O little town of Bethlehem, how still we see thee lie!
Above thy deep and dreamless sleep the silent stars go by.
Yet in thy dark streets shineth the everlasting Light;
The hopes and fears of all the years are met in thee tonight.

For Christ is born of Mary, and gathered all above,
While mortals sleep, the angels keep their watch of wondering love.
O morning stars together, proclaim the holy birth,
And praises sing to God the King, and peace to men on earth!

O holy Child of Bethlehem, descend to us, we pray;
Cast out our sin, and enter in, be born in us today.
We hear the Christmas angels the great glad tidings tell;
O come to us, abide with us, our Lord Emmanuel!

—PHILLIPS BROOKS

Away in a Manger

Away in a manger, no crib for a bed,
The little Lord Jesus laid down His sweet head;
The stars in the sky looked down where He lay,
The little Lord Jesus, asleep on the hay.

Be near me, Lord Jesus, I ask Thee to stay
Close by me forever, and love me, I pray;
Bless all the dear children in Thy tender care,
Prepare us for heaven, to live with Thee there.

—ATTRIBUTED TO MARTIN LUTHER

Little Christmas Guest

O welcome, little Christmas Guest,
Dear Jesus, from above;
Upon Your face, so pure and mild,
We see God's smile of love. Amen.

—UNKNOWN

Jesus, Our Jesus

Jesus in the manger, so far from Your throne.
Jesus in Bethlehem, a stable Your home.

Jesus in Mary's lap, a baby so small.
Jesus in Joseph's arms, asleep in the stall.

Sleep sweetly, dear Jesus,
Sleep sweetly, our King.

We'll praise You forever,
With angels we'll sing.

—MAX & DENALYN

A Savior Is Born

Today your Savior was born in David's town.
He is Christ, the Lord. This is how you will know him:
You will find a baby wrapped in cloths and lying in a
feeding box.

—LUKE 2:11–12

My Birthday

Dear God, of all the many days
That I have lived to see,
My birthday is the one of all
That most belongs to me.
This day is mine because Your love
Gives me a life to live.
I thank You, God, with all my heart
For this dear day You give.

—JOHN MARTIN

Thank You, God!

Give thanks to the Lord because he is good.
His love continues forever.

—Psalm 136:1

For Everything!

Thank You, God, for **doodlebugs** that roll in a ball.

Thank You for the forts we build out in the hall.

Thank You for **rain** and *snow* and days in the sun.

Thank You for bikes and trikes and pink **bubblegum**.

Thank You for music and *toys* and bells that ring.

Thank You, God. Yes, thank You, God, for everything!

—MAX & DENALYN

When you see the beauty of nature all around you, let it remind you to give thanks to God for the world He made.

God in Heaven

Thank You, God in heaven
For a day begun.
Thank You for the breezes,
Thank You for the sun.

For this time of gladness,
For our work and play,
Thank You, God in heaven
For another day.

—Traditional

A Song of Thanks

Dear heavenly Father, hear us sing,
    Our song of thanks for everything;
Thank You, thank You, thank You, heavenly Father.

—Author Unknown

HEAVEN

All I Have

God, You are in heaven—
You care, and You are good to me.
Yes, all I have to eat or wear,
It's You, God, who gives it to me!

—ANNE TAYLOR GILBERT, *ADAPTED*

For All I See

God, You made everything!
The tall palm trees whose leaves wave to the heavens,
The giant whales, like the one that swallowed Jonah,
And the tall ocean waves that cover the rocks,
Thank You, God, for all I see.
And thank You, God, O thank You for making me!

—MAX & DENALYN

Father of Goodness

O Father of goodness,
    We thank You each one
    For happiness, healthiness,
    Friendship and fun,
For good things we think of
    And good things we do,
    And all that is beautiful,
    Loving and true.

—PRAYER FROM FRANCE

The Appleseed Prayer

The Lord is good to me,
And so I thank the Lord.
For giving me the things I need:
The sun, the rain, and the appleseed!
The Lord is good to me.

And every seed that grows
Will grow into a tree.
And one day soon
There'll be apples there,
For everyone in the world to share.
The Lord is good to me.

—ATTRIBUTED TO JOHN CHAPMAN, "JOHNNY APPLESEED"

A Glorious Name

Now, our God, we thank you.
    And we praise your glorious name.

—1 CHRONICLES 29:13

The Bible

Jesus, thank You for the Bible:
The Bible is Your Word.
You always tell the truth;
You teach me how to live and love,
That's all I need for proof.

Help me learn as I read it today,
To trust Your words and believe what You say.
Help me to smile, inside and out;
Help me to laugh and give a big shout!

—Max & Denalyn

Thank You, Father

In the morning when I wake,
I run to the window straight,
One look at the day I take
And say, "Thank You, Father."

At the table, in my seat,
When my breakfast I begin,
For the food so good to eat
I say, "Thank You, Father."

When the sun sleeps in the west,
Mother tucks me in my bed,
Then I say, "For play and rest
Thank You, thank You, Father."

—Edith Lovell Thomas

My Daily Prayer

Lord, thank You for Your tender care,
    And all Your love to me;
The food I eat, the clothes I wear,
    Are all Your gifts to me.

My health, and friends, and parents dear,
    To me by God are given;
I have not any blessing here
    But what is sent from heaven.

Such goodness, Lord, and constant care,
    A child can never repay;
But may it be my daily prayer,
    To love You and obey.

—JANE TAYLOR GILBERT, *ADAPTED*

God Is Near

God, we thank you.
    We thank you because you are near.
We tell about the wonderful things you do.

—PSALM 75:1

I Love You, God!

Thank You for toys
    and animals
        and hugs
           and food.

Thank You for playtime
    and naptime
        and dinnertime
           and prayer time.
Thank You, God! I love You.

—Max & Denalyn

We All Thank You

God, we all thank You,
With our hearts and hands and voices;
For all the great wonders You have done,
In You this world rejoices.

—Martin Rinkart, *Adapted*

Giving Thanks

I will praise God in a song.

    I will honor him by giving thanks.

—Psalm 69:30

God, Our Creator

O God, we thank You for this earth, our home;

    for the wide sky and the blessed sun,

    for the salt sea and the running water,

    for the everlasting hills and the never-resting winds,

    for trees and the common grass underfoot.

We thank You for our senses by which

    we hear the songs of birds,

    and see the splendor of the summer fields,

    and taste of the autumn fruits,

    and rejoice in the feel of the snow,

    and smell the breath of the spring.

Grant us a heart wide open to all this beauty;

    and save our souls from being so blind that we pass unseeing

    when even the common thornbush is aflame with Your glory,

    O God our creator, who lives and reigns for ever and ever.

—Walter Rauschenbusch

GOOD NIGHT, GOD

I go to bed and sleep in peace.
Lord, only you keep me safe.

—PSALM 4:8

Life is sweeter after you rest in the Lord.

Good Night, Jesus

Jesus, You are here!
Jesus, You are strong.
Jesus, You will keep me safe
This whole night long.

Jesus, You are good.
Jesus, You are right.
Jesus, You will hold me close
All throughout the night.

Jesus, in my room.
Jesus, by my bed.
Jesus watching over me,
From my toes up to my head!

Good night, Jesus!

—MAX & DENALYN

Jesus, Tender Shepherd

Jesus, tender Shepherd, hear me;
Bless Your little lamb tonight;
Through the darkness please be near me;
Watch over me till morning light.

All this day Your hand has led me,
And I thank You for Your care;
You have warmed and clothed and fed me;
Listen to my bedtime prayer.

Let all my sins be forgiven;
Bless the friends I love so well;
Take me, Lord, one day to heaven,
Happy there with You to dwell. Amen.

—MARY LUNDIE DUNCAN, *ADAPTED*

Angels Guard Me

Lord, keep me safe this night,
Secure from all my fears;
May angels guard me while I sleep,
Till morning light appears.

—JOHN LELAND

Sleep Safe

Father God, to You I pray,
You have guarded me all day;
I am safe while in Your sight,
Safely let me sleep tonight.

Bless my friends—the whole world bless;
Help me to learn helpfulness;
Keep me always in Your sight;
Now to all I say good night.

—HENRY JOHNSTONE, *ADAPTED*

A Good Night Prayer

Now I lay me down to sleep.
I pray You, Lord, my soul to keep.
Your love be with me through the night
And wake me with the morning light.

—TRADITIONAL

Keep Me Through the Night

O, holy Father, I thank You
For all the blessings of this day.
Forgive me for all that I have done wrong.
Bless me and keep me through the night,
For Jesus' sake. Amen.

—Author Unknown

While We Sleep

Blessed Lord, we thank You
For Your care today.
Make us good and gentle,
Take our sins away.

Bless the friends who love us,
From all evil keep.
May Your holy angels
Guard us while we sleep. Amen.

—Thomas Simmons

God Is Near

I hear no voice, I feel no touch,
I see no glory bright,
But still I know that God is near
In darkness as in light.

He watches always by my side,
And hears my whispered prayer.
The Father for His little child
Both day and night does care.

—AUTHOR UNKNOWN

God Holds My Hand

Lord, when we have not any light,
And mothers are asleep,
Then through the stillness of the night
Your little children keep.

When shadows fill the quiet room,
Help us to understand
That You are with us through the gloom
To hold us by the hand.

And though we do not always see
The holy angels near,
O may we trust You and believe,
There's no need for any fears.

So in the morning may we wake,
When wakes the kindly sun,
More loving for our Father's sake
To each unloving one.

—ANNIE MATHESON, *ADAPTED*

Count the Hours

When it gets dark, the birds and flowers
Shut up their eyes and say good night;
And God, who loves them, counts the hours
And keeps them safe till it gets light.

Dear Father! Count the hours tonight,
When I'm asleep and cannot see;
And in the morning may the light
Shine for the birds and flowers and me!

—WILLIAM HAWLEY SMITH

Under Golden Wings

Dear Lord Jesus,
As a hen covers her chicks with her wings
    To keep them safe,
Protect us this dark night
    Under Your golden wings.

—A PRAYER FROM INDIA

The Moon Shines Bright

The moon shines bright,
    The stars give light
      Before the break of day.
God bless you all,
    Both great and small,
      And send a joyful day.

—TRADITIONAL

Through the Night

God, you are my God. . . .
I remember you while I'm lying in bed.
    I think about you through the night.
You are my help.
    Because of your protection, I sing.

—PSALM 63:1, 6–7

Keep Me Close

Jesus, keep me close to You
    And I won't be afraid.
I know that You are with me;
    Help me as I pray.
I give You all my fears;
    You know just what to do.
You throw my fears away
    And only speak the truth.
The truth is that You love me;
    You are always in my heart.
I never have to be afraid,
    Even in the dark.

—MAX & DENALYN

I See the Moon

I see the moon,
And the moon sees me:
God bless the moon,
And God bless me.

—TRADITIONAL

Now the Day Is Over

Now the day is over,
Night is drawing nigh,
Shadows of the evening
Steal across the sky.

Now the darkness gathers,
Stars begin to peep,
Birds and beasts and flowers
Soon will be asleep.

Jesus, give the weary
Calm and sweet repose;
With Your tender blessings
May our eyelids close.

Through the long night watches,
May Your angels spread
Their white wings above me,
Watching round my bed.

When the morning wakens,
Then may I arise
Pure, and fresh, and sinless
In Your holy eyes.

—SABINE BARING-GOULD, *ADAPTED*

My Prayer for Today

Love, joy, peace, patience, kindness, goodness,
Faithfulness, gentleness, and self-control—
That is what I will try to show today.
I pray, Lord, that You will help me.
When I mess up, please forgive my mistakes,
And cover me with Your grace.
And then, when this day is all done,
I will lay my head on my pillow
And rest.
Amen.

—Max & Denalyn

The Lord's Prayer

Our Father in heaven,
    we pray that your name will always be kept holy.
We pray that your kingdom will come.
We pray that what you want will be done,
    here on earth as it is in heaven.
Give us the food we need for each day.
Forgive the sins we have done,
    just as we have forgiven those who did wrong to us.
Do not cause us to be tested;
    but save us from the Evil One.

—Matthew 6:9–13